I0149144

All Scripture references taken from the

KJV of the Holy Bible

Money Hunters: Beware of Those Hunting Money, by
Dr. Marlene Miles

Freshwater Press 2023

ISBN: 978-1-960150-62-2

Paperback Version

Table of Contents

MONEY HUNTERS

Beware of Those Hunting Money

Freshwater

Money Hunters

Money hunters are among the most dangerous people in the world. There are people who will do anything for money. They will sell anything, sell anyone, sell anyone out. The pursuit of the money hunter is money. It is what they live for; it is *all* they live for. It's as though they are programmed and remote controlled because once they get money, they keep going and going. A money score is never enough.

The Bible warns against chasing money, indicating that those who do are destined for misery and ultimate failure, either in the physical, the spiritual realm, or both.

For to the one who pleases him God has given wisdom and knowledge and joy, but to the sinner he has given the business of gathering and collecting only to give to one who pleases God. This also is vanity and a striving after wind. Ecclesiastes 2:26

...the sinner's wealth is laid up for the righteous. Proverbs 13:22

It is not clear from the Bible if Judas was an evil money hunter, if he was jealous, hated Jesus, or if he was stupid and duped as to why Judas sold Jesus out *for* the 30 pieces of silver. Did Judas sell Jesus out for *some* money and didn't even know what he was going to get? Was 30 pieces of silver the agreed upon amount for the betrayal? Was 30 pieces of silver a lot of money at that time? It was the cost of a slave. It was the cost to be paid to the owner if someone's slave was accidentally killed.

If Judas was a money hunter, even 30 pieces of silver would not have been enough to satisfy his greed. The greed of money hunters cannot be satisfied. This is why the line in a lot of movies, *just one more heist and this will be the last one* doesn't work. Money hunters are never satisfied.

Further problems were that Judas didn't **own** Jesus, and Jesus was not Judas's slave. Neither was Judas Jesus' master so receiving the compensation for a lost slave was an insult on both ends of that deal. In addition to all the other insults, 30 pieces of silver for Jesus was a serious downgrade, attempting to demean and belittle Jesus, the **King** of *kings* to the position of slave, the lowest person in society.

We are warned not to chase after money because in God, man should never have to hunt for money, but man does a lot of things he shouldn't. He also *doesn't* do a lot of things that he <u>should</u> be doing. God has made plenty of people rich throughout all the Bible, and through the ages. You may be one of those people. God says to seek first the Kingdom and all these other things will be added unto you. God says do not store up for yourself things that can be stolen, rust, or that moth can corrupt.

Most people think that money is the key to happiness, that it is all they need to be happy. There are a lot of things that money can't buy, like love, for instance. Money is necessary, however, for life in this material world, but so is food. But we don't worship food, or we shouldn't, therefore we should not worship money, especially since it says in the Bible not to do that-, and, both money and food can come, and go.

There is only one key to a successful, healthy, and happy life, and that is God. Other than God, there is no one thing that is the key to an abundant life. Money is not all that there is, and it is not all you need. Money shouldn't be the sole focus in life, because who can take it with them? No one.

A person could have all the money that they need, but what if their health is suffering? A person could have their health, but what if they do need money? A person could have both health and money, but a person who lusts for money does not place a high value on love and may be incapable of meaningful relationships.

Talk of material goods started in Genesis, where God gave Cain and Abel instructions on gifts, offerings, and first fruits to Him. Cain and Abel were the kids of the disobedient Adam and Eve, so it might be a miracle if they obeyed God. Half of them did. Abel paid, but Cain was greedy, and appeared to want to keep that offering for Cain--, all for himself. I say that because Cain took such a long time to bring his offering to God, and when he did bring it, it was a trifling offering. Couldn't Cain realize that God is infinite and was trying to establish covenant? So Cain held on to a basket of fruit because of greed, or his image of God wasn't big enough to think that God had enough fruit to last

Cain his entire life. But, of course, God has enough; God is infinite.

In those days, offerings were for a number of things, covenant, dedication, atonement and worship. The giving of material goods and money to God is a test for man who is tempted to greed and disobedience.

We need to establish covenant with God because God is great, God is greater not just than we are, but He is also mightier than anything that could come up against us, spiritually or physically. We **need** Him for protection, for life, for everything. So we **need** to establish covenant with God. *That* He wants to establish covenant with us is a miracle and we should be eternally grateful.

We establish covenant with God, we do not make covenant with money; we should not make covenant with things, or stuff. However, that is possible, it's called a soul tie. We don't soul tie ourselves to money, although the Bible says it answers all things. Pay your bills, give, help others, but money needs to have a fluidity where it flows in and out of your hands and life.

The money and the gifts that come from you and me *represent* our blood, sweat, tears, and toil--, our life. But were it not for God giving us life and breath, we would have nothing to bring Him.

Money is *for* our life; it is not all there is **to** life. It represents life; it is not our life. It is not the only thing we live for. We, saints of God, are **not** money hunters.

God told Cain and Abel to bring certain sacrifices to Him. The OT outlines many different types of offerings. There's a burnt offering, a worship offering, grain offering, drink offerings--, that represent Thanksgiving, worship, dedication, atonement, or covenant. Among these offerings, there's a peace offering, a sin offering. The atonement offering was no longer necessary after Jesus Christ. Now, with the Better Blood, we don't need to bring in animal sacrifices or offerings.

But Man

But man, of course, has decided to take things in his own hands, do things his own twisted way. Man decides or sometimes gets tricked into serving idol *gods*. In so doing, he has to appease these idol *gods*. Oddly, idols want sacrifices, too—the same thing that God required in the Old Testament. These offerings are what God should be getting.

Instead of to God, the idolatrous man offers sacrifices to idols or false *gods* in the form of food, drinks, verbal, and other acts of worship, as well as money or goods.

We Submit Our *Own* Bodies

God required and accepted animal sacrifices in the Bible as atonement for sins until Jesus came, died for us and gave us the Better Covenant with the Better Blood. For this reason, in Christianity, we don't bring animals for sacrifice anymore.

From Romans 12 we learned that we are supposed to present our bodies, our *own* bodies as a **living** sacrifice holy and acceptable to God. In common vernacular we could say that we lay down our flesh lives, willingly to honor God. It serves mankind too, that we walk by the Spirit and not by the flesh.

In the Old Testament, when God asked Abraham to sacrifice Isaac, God was testing Abraham to see if he really trusted God. And he did. God was pleased with Abraham's faith, so He provided a ram in the bush. This was a foreshadowing of the sacrifice of Jesus Christ at Calvary, who was, like Isaac also tied to wood.

Most of us have smart kids, beautiful kids, kids that we may have even had difficulty bringing into the Earth realm. Some parents have birthed their kids later in life--, in their old age like Abraham and Sarah. In any case, we have to be careful not to worship our children.

Abraham and Sarah had Isaac at such an old age and a lengthy wait, a decades-long promise. God had to be sure that Abraham wasn't worshipping that child especially since Abraham had listened to Sarah and had sent Ishmael, and his mother, Hagar away.

So still we are to present *ourselves* as a **living** sacrifice to God.

We do not bring animals to sacrifice; God does not require that anymore, since He sacrificed His own Son. That's not done anymore. We definitely don't bring children or people to sacrifice. We do not sacrifice children to evil *gods* \--, to Molech or any other.

No one presents *us* as a sacrifice in the Kingdom of God; we present ourselves to God, alive and well, preferably whole. This is a choice of our own free will.

We need to establish covenant with God so we can **live**, and we can live more abundantly, because there is a lot coming at us on a daily basis. God says to seek first the Kingdom of Heaven and all of its righteousness, and then all these things will be added to us. So we don't need to be money hunters because money, goods, and all things that pertain to life and godliness will be provided for us. If we seek first the Kingdom, then God will trust us with the true riches if He can trust us with how we handle gifts, goods, offerings, money, and the like.

The Scripture says, *Woe unto them, that would be rich*. It also says*, If therefore, if you've not been faithful in the unrighteous Mammon, who will commit to you, the true riches?* From Scripture we also learn that if you have not been faithful in that which is another man's, who shall give you that which is your own?

Instead of handling money and goods well, all through the Bible we see that folks were stealing from each other. The thief comes not but to steal, kill and destroy. Jacob stole Esau's birthright, his inheritance, therefore his money. Laban stole from Jacob. Jezebel stole Naboth's vineyard, and so on.

Before he was named Israel which means *prince*, Jacob's name meant supplanter. A supplanter is someone is one who will take another's   place,

another's   position,   even
another's wealth and money.

Woe unto those who lust to be rich.
Do not toil to be rich. The lust for money
is the root of all evil are all familiar Bible
warnings about the pursuit of money.

How Much Money?

I can name two or three fellows that I was interested in in my college days, but I didn't get those guys. I didn't get that guy that I had my eye on because they didn't know if my daddy was rich, well connected, or someone important. But they turned their heads to the young ladies who had rich, important, or well-connected dads. Kindly, I suppose we can call those young men ambitious; but I call them money hunters.

As the song, *Summertime* goes, Summertime, and the living is easy--, your daddy's rich and your momma's good looking--, that's what money hunters are looking for. They're looking for means, they're looking for comforts, they're looking for the comfortable life. If that life comes by marrying into it, perhaps that's what they'll do. I know a man who, when he saw a young woman's parents' house, he decided that he wanted a house like that—that lifestyle. So he married the girl.

My two or three college interests may not have known what my daddy's situation was. Or maybe they found a daddy--, *her* dad--, my competitor's dad that may have been richer than mine. What money hunter will tell you, *I picked her even though you've got this, this, and that over her because of her dad, or her station in life?*

They never tell you stuff like this in the movies. In the movies and TV dramas or rom coms, they have you thinking that if you look nice and you maintain your figure, that's all you need to do to get the guy of your dreams. No one tells you that if your daddy's not rich enough, you may not.

If you don't even have a dad, as is some people's plight, you might not even be respected, but that's another whole book.

No one tells you this, and that stuff is not on your radar in your 20's. It wasn't on mine. I don't think about it now, except looking back to write this book.

So this girl, who I'm competing with for the guy of my dreams--, (and neither of us may know that we are competing against one another)--, it doesn't matter really what she looks like or much else, or as long as her dad has money, means, position or something that that money hunter, that money-hunting man wants.

Her dad can, technically, *buy* his daughter any husband she wants--, any man that's willing to be bought. So the shallow money hunters are the ones that *can be* bought. In your 20's you don't think that much about his character, just if he's cute, if you're attracted to him, and how he makes you feel. Unfortunately, that's how silly girls can be in their youth. In your 20's you probably think, hey I'm cute or whatever, so I deserve this great, handsome guy. The thought that he's a gold digger doesn't cross your mind, or the mind of most people.

Women are more accused of being gold diggers than men, but it is an equal gender call.

We thank God that we didn't get hooked up with any of the shallow types, after all. God did us a solid. Money hunters' lust for money is greater than love, assuming they are even *capable* of love.

It Hurt

Unless someone has already told you, you may not know any of this. Youthful passion is the reason that young people should seek their parent's blessings before marriage, since parents are wiser; they've been there, and done that.

A young person may be so gung-ho about dating a particular person that during the competition they may try harder and harder to win the guy. You may have changed your hair, lost weight, or gained weight. You did whatever you thought it took. Perhaps you wore more makeup or shorter skirts, tighter clothes --, all ungodly endeavors. Now the downward spiral starts, and you are now attracting something else that you never planned to attract —, downgrades, instead of upgrades. So you're really off your timeline and off your scroll that God had planned for you.

But all the while you've fixed yourself up some certain kind of way and you're hoping that you'll meet the right person and maybe you two can *build* together, whether you both have money or not, if you have means or not, position or not. At least that's what all the love songs on the radio are about. Somewhere in the back of your mind, ladies, you may struggle with the fact that *she* doesn't really look better than you do. So what's the big deal? Why is he attracted to *her*?

Don't make her an enemy. Don't obsess. Even if you do not make her an enemy, which you shouldn't; you may begin to feel inferior or insecure. We also hope that is not the case, either. Be sure you do not soul tie yourself to the fellow, even if he made all kinds of promises to you to get what he wanted from you sexually. This is one of the reasons God says not to fornicate.

(Man, the 20's can be tough.)

Flee youthful lusts. (2 Tim 2:22a)

Well, if he's a money hunter, you may not have figured out that money, the surplus of it, the lack of it, or the perception of having money was the problem. *Summertime*, and the living is easy if daddy's rich and mama's good looking.

But, in the long run, this can all be very emotionally painful, especially when you see your other college mates paired up, booed up, engaged, and even married, but not you.

We thank God that He can bind up broken hearts and heal us from rejection and all hurts.

The M.R.S. Degree

Some parents who have means, for real, or just by appearances, can *buy* their children's spouses, and they do this by sending their child to the best colleges where the best males will be.

Some looking to get married even go to professional schools and take a position that real students who **want** to practice medicine or law can't get because the spouse-seeker has one of the few slots even though they have no intention of practicing after graduating. The spouse seeker is only there to get a MRS. Degree. The parents send them there because professional school is where the *mutual money hunters* will find each other. An expensive match making service, eh?

It's hardly different in a lot of cultures. In arranged marriages no one cares what anyone *is* like or looks like. The parents may only be asking, *Do they have at least as much or more money as we do?*

Royal marriages that we see on TV, movies and in real life are similar. We have read about them in history books; they are also arranged. Royal marriages are sometimes planned at or even before birth. No one seems to care about the cousin-incest or the risk of genetic deformities in their children, they just want to keep that money and/or power in the family. Does it matter if it's a loveless marriage or if both or either party is miserable? They just want to keep that money in the family and keep up appearances.

Royal matchmaking is where parents become money hunters. Or maybe one or both of them always were. Unless

God delivers anyone, a money hunter will always be a money hunter.

You know people whose language is money. They are pretty bored unless you are talking about money. You've met people who hate you if they feel that you have cost them a dollar or made them have to spend a dollar. The types who like to split the check in restaurants and if it's an odd number, they will not pay the penny, or become angry if they have to. They will not let it go, or let it go easily. These people are money hunters; they serve Mammon.

We Have Hope

Hope springs eternal. I'm not writing any of this for any of you to give up hope; these are just things to pray about, because God can remedy all of that and make sure you end up with the right spouse, your own Kingdom spouse.

I'm telling you all this just in case you didn't think you had anything to pray about to make your life turn out right. Man ought to always pray.

Searching

Money hunters will violate pretty much any law because they don't serve the law. They serve mammon. And it's all about the money. It's all about their dollar bills, because that's their *god*. **Summertime**, and the living is easy; they want their entire life to be summertime, easy. Your mom doesn't even have to be good looking as long as your daddy is rich. Well, you know what? No matter what your parental situation is, as long as at least one of your parents is rich, well off, or comfortable, you too can win a shallow, gold digging, moneyhunting spouse.

I know a young man who's married to a demanding, much older woman. He does everything she asks him to do to the tee. When his friends ask him, *Kevin, how do you stand it? The stuff she asks you to do is ridiculous.*

He answers, *"Man, she buys me all the cars and stuff I want."* Money hunters.

Years ago I dated a man until he told me he was waiting for his rich grandmother to **die**. That was the end of that for me.

You may have met people who are checking you out, sizing you up, seeing what you got, checking for you to see if you have money because money is *their* god. They're not really looking for a *relationship* with you. They will associate with you, they may even marry you, but it seems more like they are looking for a relationship with your money. Perhaps they are looking for more money to worship. This type is often never satisfied. They don't need money, some do, some don't, but they just want more. They want more because they're never satisfied.

The questions are brazen: What kind of house do you live in? What kind of furniture do you have? Do you have TV's? Are they expensive? What kind of car do you drive? How *many* cars do you have? What is your occupation? Show me what you're working with. Send me some pics. Tell me how much money you have. Yeah, they'll even ask that. These are the true money hunters.

I once had a guy ask me if I *had* any money. I responded, *Why? Do you need some?* I wasn't going to give him any, but impertinent questions should be responded to with another question.

(You're welcome.)

Then there are people who are adorning and over-adorning themselves, as discussed earlier. But some people put too much on the outside, too much jewelry, too much makeup, too much of the most expensive cologne making a show of wealth. They may draw more attention or the wrong type of attention to themselves than they originally hoped for.

Appearances are not always true, actually.

I know a fellow who told me he saw a lady driving a certain luxury car on the Interstate, so he flirted with her from his car, while they both were driving at 70mph. Eventually they both decided to pull over at a rest stop to meet and talk. Why? They both were driving very nice late model luxury cars and they both were money hunters. When he found out that it wasn't her car and that she didn't have wealth, he was no longer interested in her.

As he was then, men today are looking for women of means, and will boldly say so. They call these *high value women*. Let's recap: the woman has to be of a high financial value, carry and give birth to all the kids, cook the meals, and clean the house. What is he doing while all this work is going on? Oh, he lives the life of leisure because he's a man. And it's summertime.

There are too many women who are buying into this because they desperately want a man, a mate, or a husband. They work extra hard to hold on to their man, to *hold their man down*, as if that man will be eternally grateful and never leave them. Please--, there is no guarantee.

It's too much. Women don't do this.

And, unmarried woman, he's out there. He's asking you all that stuff, but he's asking everybody else he meets the same stuff. He's searching for the one that's got the most, has what he wants, or is willing to give him what he wants. The lust for money will win over love every time. Even if he meets a woman he loves, money is his *god*, and he will leave her if he's a money hunter.

Beware of those looking for money.

Ladies, all this time while you are auditioning for him, what's he showing you? What's he offering you? Is this supposed to be a business deal or a relationship? Is this supposed to be a connection, or a transaction?

Today's women, come on--, you're accomplished. You've got it going on. You shouldn't have to *buy* a man because he's decided that he's a catch and you're desperate. All of this has thrown you into a masculine energy as you pursue him. You don't want to go there; you must remain feminine and a lady, as God has intended you to be. There is a kingdom spouse for you who doesn't ascribe to money hunting tactics.

If he's a money hunter, you can be outbid at any time, any day or hour.

The money hunters want to be rich and live in comfort. They want creature comforts.

I can name people right now--, I won't, but I know people, male and female--, who believe the trappings of affluence are all that's needed in life, and then they'll be happy. They are satisfied with the *appearance* of wealth, such as the certain house, the certain car, clothes, jewelry, nice vacations. As long as they look good to others, they feel content.

Money hunters.

A so-called suitor hacked into my computer and financial software to see what kind of money or savings I had. When I asked him about it, he lied. Yeah, like my computer opened all those files on their own.

Once I was set up on a blind date with a potential suitor who told me that he always wanted to marry a doctor. Bye!

So please don't think that if your family is comfortable or well off, that everyone who comes into your environment is after your money. That's not always the case, but you will stay prayerful. Right?

Equal Opportunity Evil

Don't worry. If you don't have money or means, this book is for you too. Evil is equal opportunity.

Things are about to get **really** bad; I'm about to share some hard truths. In this life, you MUST stay prayed up and be discerning.

There are people who don't have much money or any money at all. These people must be discerning, sometimes more discerning and more cautious than people with means. There are men--, not just men, but I'm gonna say men for this book--, who are money hunting with a vengeance. They don't care if the person that they've targeted has money or not, because they don't plan to take money *from* that person. They don't plan to go into business with that person, but they do plan to **make money--**, not necessarily *with* that person, but they plan to make money **because of** that person. And that person is totally unaware of the plan or plans. That person is usually an innocent, and often God-fearing, trusting individual.

I'm not talking about a business deal. I'm talking about evil spiritual tactics that people, in this country, either don't know about or know little about or fail to talk about. And that's what this book is really all about.

The beginning chapters of this book were just background.

Brace yourself.

So, this evil, money-hunting man is planning to make money off an unsuspecting woman. I'm not even talking about selling a person on the street or into sex trade. While that's a real possibility, I warn you women, be careful. If a man keeps giving you fantastic gifts but he wants NOTHING in return, he's grooming you for something sinister, usually. Accepting the gifts is the initiation. What he's initiating you into is only imagined by things that you know. But there are dark things that you may know nothing about that you are being drawn into, unknowingly.

I'm talking about the more evil person who is spiritually connected to evil and knows all kinds of evil things. Pure evil. He might go to church, he might know all the hymns and all the Books of the Bible, but you need to watch him closely even if the Holy Spirit hasn't given you any inkling, or you have any suspicions. Do your due diligence when getting to know someone. *He's too good to be true*? He's got LOTS of money, but you don't know where he got it from, or where he's getting it from. And you know he's not a drug dealer or some other "normal" everyday criminal. Eyes open. Ears open; be prayerful.

Does he have a man cave that is totally off limits to you? Have you been to his house? If he has invited you to his house, does he have a secret room that must remain locked, and you have been warned not to go in there? Does he go mystery places or take mystery trips that you can't go on? Does he have weird pets?

Ladies, this is not a candidate for a relationship. He just isn't.

You had better know about his "mysteries" before you move in or say, *I do*. You need to know what his real plans for you are.

What are his real plans for your children if you already have kids? What are his real plans for the children that you two will have together? No person is safe from a true money hunter. They will do anything, trade anything, sell anything--, even *anyone* for money.

In the natural, how many women do you know are amazed at what their husband has gambled away in a poker game???

When getting to know this new person who wants to come into your life, when he is queried, if he gets defensive, doesn't answer, or answer truthfully, you'll only know those answers by praying and listening and **hearing** God. Do not quench the Spirit; listen and hear! If a man treats you like gold and he's in a hurry to marry you, even though you *are* wonderful and it's about time somebody noticed, he might have ulterior motives.

If he treats you like gold before you marry him, and the moment you say, *I do*, he starts treating you like he *don't*—you've got a real problem. If he starts treating you (or your children) like trash or refuse, his motive is never what you thought it was from the beginning, and your motives are probably not the same as his.

Fairy tales, romance, happily ever after--, let's get our heads out of the clouds and <u>see</u>, let's *discern*, let's look at what's really happening around us. We need to discern every *spirit,* so we don't marry our enemies and become victims.

So Exotic

There's the woman who is romanticizing marrying someone from another culture. You had better find out what that culture believes in and what rituals they perform, and how women, especially women, are treated in that culture. There are TV shows and movies that make it all magical, exotic, and beautiful because it is *different*, but there's a reality. There is a spiritual reality that we as Christians, especially need to be fully aware of so we don't inherit evil and problems. Men, or women: we do not want to get initiated into something heinous that our kids will have to pay for in generations to come.

Mixed culture marriages and rites, yes, they are different and maybe lovely; what these priests are doing might be exotic, but what does God say about it? What is really happening? What are you agreeing to? What are you being initiated into? What *gods* are you <u>now</u> worshipping, or expected to worship?

Spiritually, what iniquity is in your spouse's family, and you haven't even thought of any of that because he's so cute? What are you being groomed to be a part of? Do you even know? You had better know. It beats having nightmares every night for 12 years or ruining or cursing your kids' destinies because you joined a culture that you knew little to nothing about.

Can't Buy Love

Through the ages, people who have money   seem to have more friends, well --, certainly more fake friends. Therefore, they have more enemies, because of money.

Wisdom is better than strength.
Nevertheless, the poor man's wisdom is
despised and his words are not heard.
(Ecclesiastes 9:16).

Yeah, what I said, nobody's listening to the broke guy. Money talks and *not*-money walks.

Money can buy a ticket, but money is not THE ticket; sometimes it causes problems, sometimes it brings the problems.

Ask ME

For the love of money is the root of all kinds of evil, (1 Timothy 6:10).

It is through this lust many are drawn away from the faith and spiral down into evil. The love of money is the root of all kinds of sin. The *lust* for money is the root of all evil.

Lust is a work of the flesh. If you put any work of the flesh with anything else, it will at least change that thing in a negative way. At most it may destroy its original purpose as planned by God. Money can be bad on its own, not enough or too much money can bring on problems. Not always--, but when you have the lust for it, it's supercharged for evil.

Money hunters have lust. That is why they're hunting money. There's lust and love at war again, they cannot co-exist. In the unsaved, unregenerated, un-delivered man lust will win every time. Kingdom people, God's people should move in love and never lust.

Unsaved and carnal people chase after their idols, whether they realize it, or admit it, or not. They believe that these idols will give them fame, power, and/or wealth. Some seek idols for revenge. Others believe their motives are more noble as they are seeking marriage, children and/or healing, for example. These are some of the common reasons (excuses) why people worship idols.

The real purpose of idolatry and idol worship is to get rich quicker or to get whatever you want quicker and easier than asking God. Remember, we are supposed to be seeking first the Kingdom and all of its righteousness, **then** things will be added to us.

Money hunters want the money, but they don't want the righteousness. God says, ***Ask Me and whatever you ask I will give it to you.*** We can understand that because when someone steals from you, for example, you wonder why didn't they just ask? I would have given it to him. Well, the adulterous people, the sinners, the money hunters can't ask God because they don't want to be righteous. They don't want to stop sinning. They want the sin <u>AND</u> the money.

One has to be in order with God, abiding in Him, dwelling in Him, to ask God for things. That requires righteousness and they don't want to do right. So, they're money hunting.

You are probably just like God, if someone takes something from you, you just wonder. Why didn't they just *ask* me? They didn't ask you because just like God, they'd have to look you in the eye and be honest about why they wanted or expected you to give them something. If you're in God and God's Spirit is in you, your eyes should be very hard for a sinner to look into.

Life Eternal

People want to be rich in *things*. Money hunters want to be rich in things, yet they don't mind being poor in Spirit. They want to be rich in the things of this world, but they don't care if they're poor in the things of God. Most believe they only have this one life. It's temporal and they're gonna live it to the max. Right now. But we are eternal beings. We are spirit. And we've got to answer in eternity over what we choose to do in this life.

I've met all kinds of guys who were interested in me for financial reasons. Some needed to be, but some have plenty, but want more. Sometimes they want what you have. And while women have been accused of being gold diggers for, oh--, I don't know, *forever*, gold digging is not exclusive to women. Money hunting is gold digging, but it is far more evil and sinister. It is gold digging with a demonic charge and that charge is LUST. People who lust for food do not stop eating. People who lust for alcohol become alcoholics. People who lust for sex become sexaholics. Adding this work of the flesh to the desire for money can make a person super evil and with that single, solitary, laser focused goal in mind, that person can be convinced of or talked into just about anything.

A young woman got a divorce and her male friends wanted to know, *How much did he give you in the settlement? How much did you get in the settlement?*

Another woman became widowed, and her pastor wanted to know, *How much did he leave you?* I don't even know if the body was cold yet.

There's unrighteous mammon, and it is the only idol that is set up to be a *god*. In the Bible that is the only one who's discussed as being a *god*--, a little g *god*. And people worship it all the time, whether they admit it, whether they realize it or not.

I don't believe in vows of poverty, but I also don't believe in worshipping Mammon. While money in and of itself is not so foul that you should throw it out of your hands quickly like a hot potato, it's not something to embrace and sleep with. There's nothing wrong with having enough money. There's nothing wrong with having sufficiency, even abundance, because Jesus came that we should live abundantly in this Earth. The *why* of all of this talk is that we don't know what limits anybody will go to for the things they want until they go to those lengths. And we must pray to God that we aren't or don't become one of those desperately obsessed souls, or worse, a victim of one of those evil souls.

Pray if you suspect foul, criminal, or evil money-play. If the Holy Spirit reveals foul play to you, and says, Get out, then get out! And, do it with a quickness.

Money Rituals

Evil money hunters of money will do ***money rituals.*** What are money rituals? I won't say, because the purpose is not to teach anyone what they are, but just that they exist, and they are spiritual. They are evil; trust that. And there are things that many of us wouldn't believe anyway, even if somebody told us, or if you saw it with your own eyes.

These things are not only damaging to the victim, but they may also be deadly. We're to offer our own bodies as a living sacrifice. We are not to *be* someone else's sacrifice. If you didn't think you had anything to pray for, pay attention, because we do not know what lengths anyone will go to for what they want until they go to those lengths--, such as animal sacrifice.

Idolatrous wicked altars want blood, whether animal sacrifice, or even human sacrifice. Sexual fluids have DNA in them and are considered as blood sacrifices. This is why we don't spill seed. God hates spilled seed. This is why we all must keep up with our own bodily fluids-- always, no matter what time of the month it is. There are people trying to use these fluids for all kinds of evil, such as an evil exchange. Ladies, the fornicating man who ONLY wants to see you at certain times of the month?

The man that you are dating, but no matter what time of the month it is, as soon as you talk with him or see him suddenly your menses starts. Is he upsetting you *that much*? Does he pick fights all the time to keep you upset? **He could be out for blood,** without killing you, of course. He could be doing or have done money rituals. Demons want blood--, animal or even human.

There are many kinds of spiritual dangers, even after we are saved. Stay prayed up against things such as destiny exchange. There are star hunters out there. There are virtue stealers. You have to possess your vessel in sanctification and honor. I used to think that only meant that you had to behave yourself in a Godly way. It does mean that, but it means to protect everything valuable that God has given you, including your body and every part of it as well as your soul and spirit. That is done spiritually, by prayer and relationship, covenant with God. Not by might, but by the Spirit. Stay. Prayed. Up.

Sex magic is a real thing, people of God. Did you not know it? You wouldn't be too quick to do anything sexual with anyone other than your covenanted Kingdom spouse, if you knew about these things because people can use your willingness to engage randomly, intimately with them against you in amazing, and unbelievable, hateful, evil ways to their benefit, and to your detriment. They don't care; they are money hunters. They are transactional, money hunters.

They don't want your friendship; they want your money. Just as many pan handlers don't want the sandwich that you were going to eat for lunch when they said they were hungry. They don't want that sandwich, they want money.

A fake girlfriend once told me the story of having nothing to give her teen for Christmas. I wasn't working then, myself, but I thought it would be decent of me to ship her two brand new sweaters several states away, that I had gotten for myself. Even though she and I had talked about these sweaters, she didn't want those sweaters; she wanted the money. Once she received them, she asked me for the receipts because she didn't like the *styles*. No, that didn't happen. She wanted the money.

That was a lot more mundane than a money ritual, but money hunters want the money. If a money hunter has done a money ritual that involves sex; they don't even want the sex; it is a means to an end. They want the money. If a hook-up or person has SCRIPTED the act, whether in the name of "role play" or not, and you are told to say certain words at certain times, suspect that a money ritual is involved.

Can you see now why it is not wise to fornicate? Many times, parents tell us things that are for our protection; God is our parent. He says don't fornicate. Besides defiling themselves, risking hell if they don't repent, fornicators lose on so many different levels.

Asmodeus

Money hunters come to steal, but some of them don't mind killing and destroying in the process, like the robbers who don't intend to kill, but they brought guns, anyway.

Their real goal is the money, not the girl, and not the guy--, not a relationship with romance, and happily ever after, but the money. You need to be on the lookout. Be prayerful but keep your eyes open. Be discerning. Listen, pay attention. A person who is obsessed with money may either be a money hunter, or they are likely to become one.

Some signs that a person is obsessed with money are, all they talk about is money. They may forego having certain necessary, important things in life to try to get rich. They work all the time, money-grubbing instead of being home, spending time with their spouse and family. People who resort to cons and crime, rip-offs and scams are also obsessed with money. All these types are transactional, and they don't really care that much about people, they care about money and/or their appearance of success. If you've come upon this type, you should run. Unless you're just like that--, then repent. If you are not like that, you should run when a person who will scorch the Earth for a dollar comes into your life.

You're made out of Earth. You don't want to be scorched, so you should run. You should run.

The money-obsessed person jumps into every get rich scheme that comes their way. They enter chance lotteries all the time.

People of God, lotteries, raffles, sweepstakes, and drawings are lorded over by a demon named. Asmodeus.

Asmodeus is the king of lust. Anyone who enters lotteries, raffles, sweepstakes, and drawings, *especially Christians*, take note. You cannot justify playing the Lottery, no matter how tempting the multimillion-dollar prizes are by saying, *It's only a dollar or two, and if I win, I'm going to do all kinds of good in the world.*

Saints of God, do you know what you just did? You are not just playing the Lottery; you are being **played** by the Lottery. You just signed yourself up to serve that little g *god*, Asmodeus by putting that dollar or $2 on his altar. That was a form of worship. You just initiated yourself into this evil Kingdom. You just made **covenant** with the demon, Asmodeus.

(I know, why didn't someone tell us this before now? The Lottery is so commonplace and seems so innocent.) It is gambling. There is a reason gambling is so addictive, it is ruled over by a demonic *spirit*. It charges the emotions. I know people who get so excited when they win, hyped, stoked--, it's a demonic charge whether they realize it or not. The gambling *spirit*/demon Asmodeus wants worship. That *spirit* wants your dollar, or two, or ten, or fifty or $100, or whatever you are willing or duped into spending to try to win the jackpot because that money is an offering and with that money, **covenant** is established. That little bit of money is a means to an end; Asmodeus wants your soul.

Covenant with the demons means **that demon now has the right to move in and out of your life**, even your *body* at will. Covenant gives that demon access to your soul.

Gamblers have broken marriages. Wonder why. Gamblers have drinking problems. Wonder why. Et cetera. All that evil and destruction travels with Asmodeus. A person could even win a million dollars, but something else in their life may fall apart. Worse, they could lose someone they **love** in connection with the "*win*" and not even realize that someone was SACRIFICED because of you. Dangerously, dangerous people say they'd give anything for _____. If you are in a relationship with a demon, such as Asmodeus, how do you know he won't go out and get that thing you want in exchange for something *he* wants? Like blood? Worship? A sacrifice?

Being in connection, association, "relationship" with money hunters is dangerous. You need to know who a man's idols are and what is his relationship to those idols – how tight they are, how invested, obsessed or possessed he is if you're going to deal with that person.

Money – depending on how a person gets it could bring on a plethora of problems.

You may have spent $10 on the lottery last week, you put $5 in the church offering. God's not answering, it seems, so you go back to the Lottery counter to play again. There are at least two problems here. In our culture, the Lottery is presented as a *game*, but the demon ruling over it is **not** *playing* with you, and a double minded man can expect to receive **nothing** from God. A third problem is you don't seem to know spiritual rules.

Asmodeus is the prince of demons and Hell, and he promotes lust of all kinds. It is said that Asmodeus may have command over up to 72 legions of demons that are responsible for torture, lust, murder, divorce, among other evils.

Asmodeus hates godly marriages, and he's responsible for gambling. He wants to possess people, especially women, so they remain single. He will even kill their husbands.

Asmodeus will sleep with anyone-- that is, he will inspire someone under his *possession*, under his power to have sex with anyone--, anyone. He hates family.

Other traits of a person being obsessed with money is that they are constantly comparing their finances to other people. They could also be cheap and penny pinching, miserly. There's no balance in their life of being a saver and being a spender. They never feel like they have enough, they're always lusting for more, they are most likely obsessed with money.

I knew a guy that if we were walking along the street and if I saw a quarter on the sidewalk, and picked it up, by the end of that day he would **need** that quarter for something or other. *Oh, I don't have any change. didn't you have a quarter?* If he thought I had money, he

64

wanted it. That's a *spirit*; that's not even a normal human behavior.

Lusting is a form of **torture** but the one lusting often doesn't realize that they are being tortured. At first, they may think this is exciting; they feel so *alive* while on their way to spiritual death. Finally, when it gets far gone, they may realize it's too much, and may seek deliverance. When they don't have money or they feel like they don't have enough money, they're miserable, miserly, desperately cutting corners, penny-pinching, worried, and tormented. They are miserable. Even if they don't even *need* any money, they just want more or are lusting, that is driven to go out and score money, again.

Lusting involves the *spirit of dissatisfaction*. A person could already have the thing they are lusting for, but are either not satisfied with it, or feel that it is not enough. That's why gamblers may win, but they "play it all back." They lose all they "won" because they want more. That's frustration; more torture.

When money or a lack of it affects your mood, then you're obsessed with money. A girl said that her grandmother told her that you're never hungry until you don't have any money in your pocket.

You're fascinated with money if you're fascinated with people who have money just because they have money. This is the source of a lot of celebrity worship.

If you are a person who pretends to have more money than you do, you're probably obsessed with money. You could have a bunch of dollar bills and fold a $100 bill on top to make it look like you've got a wad of Benjamins that you take out in front of people from time to time. Stop it. Stop it.

If you worship people who have money, or you nearly worship them and you're angry and hate people who have money, you're probably obsessed with money.

Strange Things

There are people who will likely do strange things with money. They may do strange things to *get* money. As I said, you wouldn't believe some of the rituals that people do. To be wise, you have to look for the danger signs. You cannot wait until stuff happens to you because by that time it might be too late spiritually, as well as in the natural.

Some of the things people do for money is hunt for souls to sell. A spiritually uncovered person could be dedicated against their will and without their knowledge to Evil. How this is all done is not the scope of this book. Just know that it is done. Physical and spiritual body parts are put up for sale-- . Ladies, your reproductive parts are especially valuable in evil spiritual circles. I'm talking money hunters here, and they may look like your everyday folks. They may even look **better** than your everyday person. They may be rich, rich, rich.

STAY. PRAYED. UP.

In the natural your hair, the dirt under you shoes, your fingernails or other excrements can be collected and sold to people who trade, barter and operate in that sort of thing. Keep up with your body excretions and fluids.

Prayers Against Money Hunters & Thieves

We're gonna pray now. We're gonna pray prayers against people who want to steal from you, who want to trick you, rob you, or even sacrifice you, or parts of you for money because they are money hunters.

Mighty God, Lion of the Tribe of Judah, Jehovah Sabaoth, King of Kings and Lord of Lords, thank You for hearing our prayers today, in the Name of Jesus.

Lord, I repent of every sin against You. Please forgive me, and remove all iniquity, in the Name of Jesus. I renounce and denounce every evil covenant made by me or my ancestors and break them by the Blood of Jesus. Lord, bind every demon assigned to enforce every curse that has resulted from bloodline sins, in Jesus' Name.

Deliver me from evil human persecutors and from evil money hunters, in Jesus' Name.

Deliver me from my enemies, O my God; protect me from those who rise up against me; deliver me from those who work evil and save me from bloodthirsty men.

For behold, they lie in wait for my life; fierce men stir up strife against me. For no transgression or sin of mine, they run and make ready.

Awake, come to meet me, and see! You, Lord God of hosts are God of Israel.

Rouse yourself to punish all the nations; spare none of those who treacherously plot evil. *Selah.*

Each evening they come back, howling like dogs and prowling about the city.

There they are, bellowing with their mouths with swords in their lips—for *"Who,"* they think, *"will hear us?"*

But you, O Lord, laugh at them; you hold all the nations in derision.

O my Strength, I will watch for you, for you, O God are my fortress.

My God in his steadfast love will meet me; God will let me look in triumph on my enemies.

My God will let me look and triumph on my enemies. Amen. (Psalm 59)

Lord, I repent, and I renounce money worship. I repent of making Mammon a *god.*

Lord, renew a right spirit in me, forgive me and give me a right attitude toward money. Give me enough that I do not want.

Lord, I repent of greed and gambling, not trusting You, but trusting in myself, or trusting in idols, trusting luck, chance, Mammon.

Lord, forgive me if I've sold anyone out or even tried to be evil in that way.

Lord, forgive me, in the Name of Jesus.

I renounce and denounce any money ritual including sex magic and repent of it, in the Name of Jesus.

Divorce Asmodeus

(prayer by Dr. Daniel Duvall)

Father in Heaven. I come before You in the mighty Name of Jesus Christ and I renounce Asmodeus and serve him a bill of divorce.

I pull up all hidden documents detailing every covenant contract entangling us and command that they be stamped with the Blood of Jesus, in the Name of Jesus.

I pray that Your heavenly host would be put on assignment to place every part of me that is loyal to Asmodeus on temporary lockdown. I pray that those parts would be put to sleep.

I now deed Asmodeus's territory in me over to the Kingdom of God and I invite You, Lord to take the Throne and begin to rule over this territory with Your rod of iron in the name of Jesus.

I now bind all gatekeepers and discover each and every   portal access   point belonging   to Asmodeus' realm and his inheritance.

I place the Blood of Jesus upon every portal access point, and I seal them with the Holy Spirit. I declare that they are put to sleep and permanently deactivated. From this day forward I take the Sword of the Spirit which is the Word of God and I cut myself free from Asmodeus' realm and his inheritance, in Jesus' name.

I return every form of counterfeit inheritance inclusive of promised wealth, position, status, calling, ability, power, genetic code, seed and any other form of counterfeit inheritance in Jesus' name. I refuse it and sever myself from it and from this day forward I choose to receive all my inheritance in Jesus Christ.

I renounce all spirit children related to Asmodeus and undo all quantum entanglements involved in their creation. I commend their judgment in the purging of the realms they occupy by judgment through Living Water. I also reclaim every part of me that has been imprisoned by Asmodeus or in his realm.

I appeal to justice according to Galatians 6:7, which declares that as a man sows, so shall he reap.

I pray that Asmodeus would now repay 100-fold return for all the evils sown against me, my ancestors, and all whom I represent in the form of justice and judgment and wrath, arrows and lightning, hailstones, tsunamis of living water and plundering by the armies of heaven in Jesus' name.

I now take authority over every evil spirit on the inside of me and around me that has been operating under the authority of

Asmodeus. I declare that you are discovered and apprehended, bound, pierced through, and thrust out of me for judgment.

I declare that you are being sent to the abyss for a failed assignment.

Lastly, I pray that every spiritual object, tattoo, device, label, marker, power source, greater branding placed in or around every part of me by Asmodeus or those under his authority would be consumed in the Holy Fire of Jesus Christ and totally dissolved.

Lord Jesus, I pray that you would cause Asmodeus' memory to perish regarding every part of me and my seed. Asmodeus, lose my location, forget my name and coordinates, in the name of Jesus.

Amen.

Warfare

Lord, I bind all Satanic powers working against me now, in the Name of Jesus.

I break all soul ties between myself and every evil *spirit* and bind them from working against me right now, in the Name of Jesus.

I bind the *spirits of greed, dissatisfaction, restlessness, barrenness, desert spirit, barren womb, pride, destruction, takeover spirit, the spirit of Absalom, locusts, uncontrolled passion, lust, fire which consumes, destroyer.*

Burning with passion, rejection, adultery, fornication, king of evil spirits, treacherousness, prince of demons, impetuousness, impatience, desperation, feasible impunity, lord of the flies, psychic and telepathic activities, Satan, jealousy, chief of demons, religious spirit, veil, extremes and excesses, lord of heaven, spiritual death, prince of scorpions, lust of the eyes, pride of life, pride of the flesh, torture, rage, Abaddon, matrimonial discord, Asmodeus. Apollyon, in the Name of Jesus, thank You, Lord,

Father. Thank You for Your loving kindness, Your Grace and Mercy and protection over my life against all the whims of the devil, in the Name of Jesus.

Father, I come against every spiritual thief and deceiver operating in my life, in the Spirit and in the natural, in the Name of Jesus.

Lord, forgive me if I am a thief. Lord, give me opportunity to redeem myself to You, because You hate robbery, in the Name of Jesus.

Father, I come against spiritual thieves operating in my dream life and also in my physical life, in the Name of Jesus,

Father, every spiritual thief and deceiver of my family that is operating against my life and destiny, I separate myself from them by the Blood of Jesus, in the mighty Name of Jesus.

Father, every spiritual thief that stole from my father that is now trying to steal from me, is stealing, or has stolen from me, I decree the Blood of Jesus is against them, in the Name of Jesus.

Lord, every spiritual money hunter that has come into my life as a friend, acquaintance, a fake friend, and especially as a suitor, I decree that they must leave me alone and leave my life immediately, in the Name of Jesus. And I declare they must repay all they have stolen and taken from me, in the Name of Jesus. Lord, put a sword between me and them now, in the Name of Jesus.

Thank You, Lord, by the Blood of Jesus, I retrieve every organ or body part from any and every evil altar, and I take it back. I take back its dedication to evil and for evil, lustful, greedy use, in the Name of Jesus.

By the Blood of Jesus I rewind, and I **undo** any initiation into any evil covenant, ritual, or curse, whether I did it knowingly or unknowingly, in the Name of Jesus.

Any part of me that is being used or was ever used or ever intended for use in any moneymaking scheme in the spirit I nullify, cancel, break, terminate, and recover every fragment, every organ, every cell, every bodily fluid, in the Name of Jesus. Lord, cleanse me with the Living Water.

I forbid the use of any part of me, any image, likeness or anything that represents me on any evil altar, in any evil dedication, for any money, ritual, curse, or spell, in the Name of Jesus.

Lord, send Your mighty warrior angels to free me from all captivity, in the Name of Jesus. Lord, I cry mercy. Mercy. I cry for mercy, Lord, in the Name of Jesus.

Lord, let whoever deceived me, used me, or has stolen from me, especially those appearing as friends, suitors, or family, let them receive the eternal judgment of God, now, in the Name of Jesus.

Father, I claim the Blood of the Eternal Covenant upon every ancestral thief operating in my life and destiny, in the mighty Name of Jesus.

I break up every evil ancient ancestral altar with the Thunder Hammer of God, in the Name of Jesus. (X3, or more)

Father, release the Fire the Holy Ghost upon every spiritual thief in my dreams and the judgment of God against every physical thief, trickster, and deceiver, in the Name of Jesus.

Lord, thank You for Your mercy and Your loving kindness toward me.

Every evil entity, power, or human persecutor seeking to gain promotion, wealth, riches, money, or fame from the Dark World. I am not your candidate. I am not your sacrifice. I am not your offering, neither me, nor my spouse, nor anyone in my family or bloodline, in the Name of Jesus.

Anytime my name or my spouse's name, or any family member, who is not under the judgment of God, is called for evil, Blood of Jesus, answer for us, in the Name of Jesus.

Thank You for Your Mercy. Do not let any resident or household evil or unrepentant evil, human persecutor hide behind the Name of Jesus, the Blood of Jesus, the Bible, or under the wings of the Almighty or His angels, in the Name of Jesus.

Thank You, Lord. Father, scatter every gang up of spiritual thieves against my life and destiny, in the mighty Name of Jesus.

Lord, scatter every money-making scheme, be it natural, physical, spiritual, or energetic, in the Name of Jesus.

Every entity, human or otherwise, with ulterior motives against my life, Lord, stop them in their tracks, turn them away from me now, in the Name of Jesus.

Father, judge every little g, *god* of the land that has sent spiritual thieves into my physical life, career, family, life and or marital destiny, in the Name of Jesus.

Father, let Your wrath consume every spiritual thief that is stealing or has come to steal the virtue or glory of my destiny, in the mighty Name of Jesus Christ.

Father, let Your wrath consume every spiritual thief that is stealing or has come to steal fortune or glory from my destiny, in Jesus's Name. (X3)

Lord, empower me to fully possess my vessel in sanctification and honor so I am not torn, fragmented, used, abused, held captive, deceived, or sacrificed in any way, in the Name of Jesus.

Lord, separate me from every human persecutor, in the Name of Jesus. Tie them down in the Spirit so they are not available to pursue me or do any harm to me, forever, in the Name of Jesus. Have them forget my name and lose my location.

Father, surround my life and destiny with Holy

Ghost Fire so that spiritual thieves won't be able to penetrate it, so they will not be able to steal from me ever again, in the Name of Jesus.

Father, I decree death upon every stranger of the night, every night raider, every *spirit spouse,* and every evil human persecutor that steals from me while I'm asleep, in the Name of Jesus.

Father, stop all money hunters in their tracks and have them turn away from me now, in the Name of Jesus.

Lord, make a wall of Fire that is too hot for the enemy to penetrate so they cannot get to me, in the Name of Jesus.

Father, I cover my life and destiny with the precious Blood of Jesus Christ against all marauders of my destiny, day or night, in the Name of Jesus.

Lord, make me unattractive to money hunters who are looking for a target for their wickedness.

Make me uninteresting to them. Make them afraid of me, in the Name of Jesus.

Lord, make me wise and discerning so that I do not succumb to any of the tricks, tactics, deceits, or initiations of evil money hunters, in the Name of Jesus.

Lord, by the power of Your Spirit render any money ritual that involves any part of me, or my life ineffective and impossible, and let me escape, unharmed, in the Name of Jesus.

Lord, by the power of Your Spirit render any money ritual that involves any part of anyone in my bloodline, ineffective and impossible, Blood of Jesus, let us escape unharmed, in the Name of Jesus.

Father, release Your mighty warrior angels to assist all escape from any and all Evil, in the Name of Jesus.

I call forth Holy Ghost Hail Stones to bombard and pulverize every spiritual thief who was sent out against my success, dealing in soul trade or any evil exchange, in my life to include marriage, family, career, and prosperity, in Jesus' Name.

Father, every deal that my forefathers made that brought about spiritual thieves into my lineage, break those evil covenants now, in Jesus' Name.

Father, by Your Word, thank You that You've built a fortress for me to protect me from evil night raiders, marauders, thieves, killers, stealers, those who come to destroy, in the Name of Jesus.

Thank You for the hedge of Fire, wall of protective Fire around my life and destiny against all those stealing from my life, in the Name of Jesus.

Father, cause my voice to sound like that of the angels, and let every spiritual thief against my life and destiny hear it, and be afraid. Let them be very afraid, in the Name of Jesus.

Father, let every spiritual thief that has stolen return all they've stolen from me at least sevenfold and have them steal no more, in Jesus' Name.

Father, by Your Word, I decree, and I declare that I am no longer a candidate for spiritual thieves. I am not a candidate for offerings or sacrifice. I am not a candidate for any evil sacrifice, worship, or any ritual, in the Name of Jesus.

Father, every agent of the devil that has been sent to rob me both physically and spiritually, let them be burned by the Fire of the Holy Ghost, in the Name of Jesus.

Father, let there be at least a sevenfold restoration of my blessings that spiritual thieves have stolen from me, in the mighty Name of Jesus Christ.

Father, release Your angels to pursue the enemies of my life and recover **all**. Have them bring back all that the devil and spiritual thieves have taken from me, in the mighty Name of Jesus Christ.

Lord, heal all the hurts, the pains, the aches, the trauma, the broken hearts, the hurt feelings and emotions from this and all other ordeals like this, in the Name of Jesus. Restore my spirit and soul.

Father, You are the Lion of the Tribe of Judah, *ROAR*! from Your heavenly throne and scatter spiritual thieves sent against me and restore me all they've stolen from me, multifold, in the Name of Jesus.

Father, by Your power I renounce and repent of whatever I ate either in the dream or the physical which was used as an instrument to bring spiritual thieves into my life.

By Your Word, I vomit up whatever's been projected into me that renders me powerless when spiritual thieves come and attack me in my dreams. Lord, I vomit it up. It comes up and out, up and out, up and out, in the Name of Jesus.

Father, I decree, and I void everything every spiritual thief and deceiver has declared over me, in the Name of Jesus.

Even though they declared war against me and have been trying to steal from my life, You are mightier than I am, mightier than they are, mightier than everyone and everything, Mighty God.

There's nothing too great for You, Lord, the King of Glory. Open up ye gates, the King of Glory is coming in, the Lord Sabaoth. Jehovah Sabaoth the Lord, mighty in battle.

Thank You, Lord, for all answered prayer, in the mighty Name of Jesus Christ, and deliver me
speedily.

Lord, be my rock of refuge, a fortress, be a defense to save me, for You are my Rock and my Fortress.

Lord, lead me and guide me. Pull me out of the net which they have secretly laid for me.

For you are my strength, Lord, You are my strength. Into your hand I commit my spirit.

You have redeemed me, Lord God of Truth, thank You.

I bind every retaliatory and payback demon, power and principality, in the Name of Jesus.

I seal these declarations across every realm, every timeline, every dimension, every age, era, past, present and future to Infinity, in the Name of Jesus. Amen.

Dear Reader

Thank you for buying and reading this book. I pray that it has enlightened and strengthened you.

May the Lord break you out of every captivity and may He restore you *at least* sevenfold, all that you have lost and all that has been taken from you. Even **_time,_** as He restores the years. In the Name of Jesus, Amen.

Dr. Marlene Miles

Other books by this author

AK: The Adventures of the Agape Kid

AMONG SOME THIEVES

Ancestral Powers

Blindsided: *Has the Old Man Bewitched You?*

Churchzilla, The Wanna-Be, Supposed-to-be Bride of Christ

Demons Hate Questions

Devil Weapons: Unforgiveness, Bitterness,...

Dream Defilement

Don't Refuse Me, Lord (4 book series)

Every Evil Bird

Evil Touch

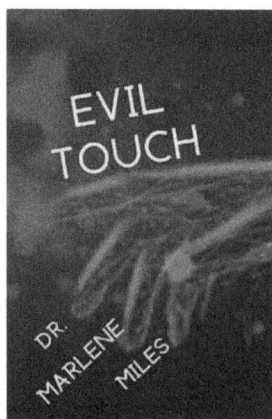

Fantasy Spirit Spouse

FAT Demons (The): *Breaking Demonic Curses*

The Fold (4 book series)

The Fold (Book 1)

Name Your Seed (Book 2)

The Poor Attitudes of Money (3)

Do Not Orphan Your Seed got HEALING? Verses for Life got LOVE? Verses for Life got HOPE? Verses for Life got money?

How to Dental Assist

Let Me Have A Dollar's Worth

Living for the NOW of God

Lose My Location

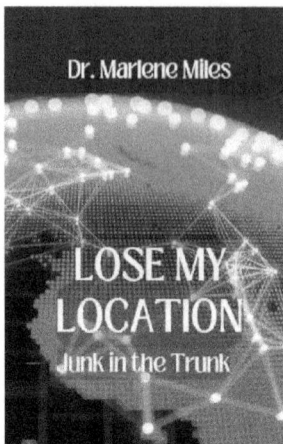

Man Safari, *The*

Marriage Ed. Rules of Engagement & Marriage

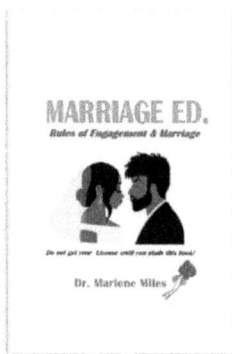

Made Perfect in Love

Motherboard (The)- soul prosperity series

Plantation Souls

Power Money: Nine Times the Tithe

The Power of Wealth *(forthcoming)*

Rules of Engagement & Marriage

Seasons of Grief

Seasons of War

Soul Prosperity soul prosperity series 3

Souls Captivity soul prosperity series 2

The Spirit of Poverty

This Is NOT That: How to Keep Demons from Coming At You

Throne of Grace: Courtroom Prayer

Time Is of the Essence

Too Many Wives: *Why You Have Lady Problems*

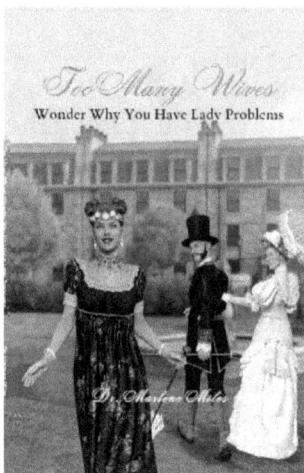

Tormenting Spirits

Triangular Power *(series)*

Powers Above

SUNBLOCK

Do Not Swear by the Moon

STARSTRUCK

Upgrade: How to Get Out of Survival Mode

Toxic Souls (Book 2 of series)

Legacy (Book 3 of series)

Warfare Prayer Against Beauty Curses
Warfare Prayer Against Poverty

When the Devourer is Rebuked

The Wilderness Romance *(series)*

- *The Social Wilderness*
- *The Sexual Wilderness*
- *The Spiritual Wilderness*

Notes: